One Big Community

Fabiola Sepulveda

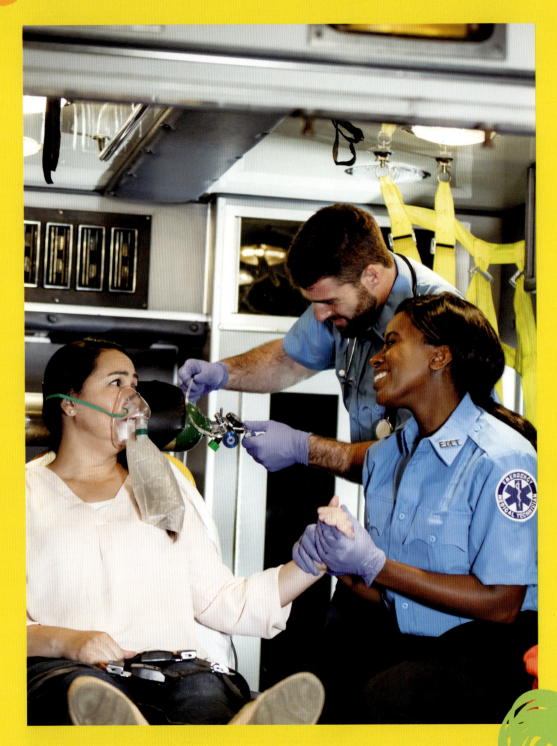

Notes for the Grown-ups

This wordless book allows for a rich shared reading experience for children who do not yet know how to read words or who are beginning to learn. Children can look at the pages to gather information from what they see, and they can suggest text to tell the story.

To extend this reading experience, do one or more of the following:

Together, list all the other people you can think of who make up a community.

Share ideas together about how people in a community might help each other.

After reading the pictures, come back to the book again and again. Rereading is an excellent tool for building literacy skills.

Introduce vocabulary such as these words when looking at the pictures and telling the story you see:

- cashier
- clerk
- coach
- community
- cook
- doctor
- crossing guard
- families
- firefighter
- grocer
- helper
- librarian
- mail carrier
- nurse
- people
- police officer
- ranger
- teacher

Discuss the people in the book and what roles in a community they play. Consider that the people shown doing jobs also have lives outside of their work.

Consultant
Cynthia Malo, M.A.Ed.

Publishing Credits
Rachelle Cracchiolo, M.S.Ed., *Publisher*
Emily R. Smith, M.A.Ed., *SVP of Content Development*
Véronique Bos, *VP of Creative*
Dona Herweck Rice, *Senior Content Manager*

Image Credits: all images from iStock and/or Shutterstock

Library of Congress Cataloging in Publication Control Number:
2024013630

This book may not be reproduced or distributed in any way without prior written consent from the publisher.

5482 Argosy Avenue
Huntington Beach, CA 92649
www.tcmpub.com
ISBN 979-8-7659-6133-9
© 2025 Teacher Created Materials, Inc.
Printed by: 926. Printed in: Malaysia. PO#: PO11723